Shadows of the Neanderthal

Illuminating the Beliefs
That Limit Our Organizations

by David Hutchens

illustrated by Bobby Gombert

PEGASUS COMMUNICATIONS, INC.
Waltham

Shadows of the Neanderthal: Illuminating the Beliefs That Limit Our Organizations
by David Hutchens; illustrated by Bobby Gombert
Copyright © 1999 by David Hutchens
Illustrations © Pegasus Communications, Inc.

Library of Congress Cataloging-in-Publication Data
Hutchens, David, 1967–
Shadows of the Neanderthal: illuminating the beliefs that limit our organizations /
by David Hutchens ; illustrated by Bobby Gombert. –1ˢᵗ ed.
p.   cm.
ISBN 1-883823-30-7
1. Creative ability in business. 2. Business communication. 3. Organizational learning.
2. I. Title
HD53.S48   1998
658.4—DC21   98-34524
CIP

Acquiring editor: Kellie Wardman O'Reilly
Project editor: Lauren Johnson
Production: Julie Quinn

♻ Printed on recycled paper.
Printed in the United States of America.
First edition

Shadows of the Neanderthal
Volume Discount Schedule
1–4 copies $19.95 each • 50–149 copies $13.97 each
5–19 copies $17.96 each • 150–299 copies $11.97 each
20–49 copies $15.96 each • 300⁺ copies $9.98 each

Prices and discounts are subject to change without notice.

Pegasus Communications, Inc. is dedicated to providing resources that help people
explore, understand, articulate, and address the challenges they face in managing
the complexities of a changing world. Since 1989, Pegasus has worked to build a
community of systems thinking and organizational development practitioners
through newsletters, books, audio and video tapes, and its annual
Systems Thinking in Action® Conference and other events.
For more information, contact us at:

Orders and Payments Offices:
PO Box 2241
Williston, VT 05495 USA
Phone: (800) 272-0945 / (802) 862-0095
Fax: (802) 864-7626
Email: customerservice@pegasuscom.com

Editorial and Administrative Offices:
One Moody Street
Waltham, MA 02453-5339
Phone: (781) 398-9700
Fax: (781) 894-7175
Email: info@pegasuscom.com

www.pegasuscom.com

05 04 03 02 01 00   10 9 8 7 6 5 4 3
5342

Chapter 1:
In Which the Cave People Ponder Their Existence

Once upon a time, there were five cave people.

Their names were
Unga, Bunga,
Oogie, Boogie,
and Trevor.

They lived together in a cave.

In fact, the cave people never left the cave. They just stayed there, day in and day out, waiting for dead bugs and dried leaves to blow in so that they might have something to eat.

The cave people embraced this isolated lifestyle. That's because they believed that the mouth of the cave was the edge of the universe.

This situation produced some interesting existential reflections among the cave people.

"Outside of cave is nothing. Go outside and *poof*—no more Unga," preached Unga.

"No, outside is big dragon. Dragon swallow Bunga whole," countered Bunga.

"No, no, no," said Oogie. "Outside is big mad god. Big mad god stomp on Oogie, and *splat*. Big gross mess."

Despite their theological differences, the cave people were united on this one point: They must never leave the cave.

In fact, just to be safe, the cave people never even *faced* the mouth of the cave. They lived their entire lives with their backs turned to the entrance.

As you can imagine, life was pretty dull for the small clan. And their backs were always sunburned.

Sometimes, an animal would pass by the front of the cave. But the cave people would never see it. Instead, with their backs turned, they would only see the animal's shadow projected onto the cave's back wall.

To the cave people, these shadows were reality.

Thus, if a hyena came leaping by the mouth of the cave, the cave people would cower from its shadow on the back wall.

Or if a butterfly drifted by, they would leap up in delight and chase its delicate, fluttering shadow.

Once, a crazed giraffe stomped a warthog to death just outside the cave.

Nobody could figure out *what* the heck *that* was.

The cave people never realized how limited
their understanding of the world was.

For them, it was just truth.
And they were satisfied.

Chapter 2:
In Which Boogie Asks a Question That Freaks Out Everyone Else

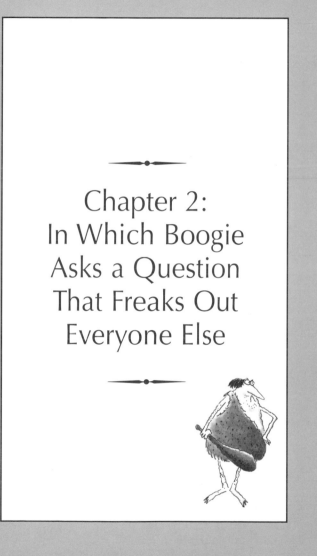

Every year as springtime rolled around, the cave people looked forward to another long, productive season in the cave, painting stick figures on the walls, eating dead bugs, and sculpting ashtrays out of clay. (Yes, ashtrays. The evolving race had yet to master the art of pottery. Thus, despite their best efforts, everything they made came out looking like an ashtray.)

Yet on one soft Spring morning, Boogie woke up feeling restless.

"Boogie bored and hungry," he said, chewing a dried magnolia leaf that had blown into the cave.

Looking around the same old drab walls of the cave, he casually mused, "Boogie wonder what is outside cave."

The others stared at Boogie in shocked disbelief.
No one had ever said such a thing before.

Boogie tried to explain: "Boogie just wonder if
maybe more food outside. Or maybe more water.
Or more room."

"What Boogie talking about?" asked Unga,
incredulous.

"*Plenty* room here!" snapped Bunga.

"And plenty food," added Trevor, sucking on a rock.

"But we only see what inside cave," Boogie said.

"What if we not see what really is?"

This question was very disturbing to the other cave people. They began to get angry.

"Boogie saying we wrong!" cried Unga.

"Boogie lost mind!" said Bunga.

"Boogie delusional and narcissistic," concluded Trevor, who often soothed his own insecurities by labeling others with sweeping psychotherapeutic generalities.

"Boogie want to ruin everything!" accused Oogie. "This could be end of us!"

"If Boogie so curious," snarled Unga, "then Boogie can just get out of cave! Go out into nothing and go *poof!*"

"Let mad god squish you like bug!" hissed Oogie.

"Go out and get breathed on by dragon's bad breath!" yelled Bunga.

Trevor picked up a clay ashtray from the ground and threw it at Boogie. The others joined in, bombarding the shocked little cave man.

"Yes, go!" they chanted. "Get out!"

Covering his head and cowering from the bruising
objects and stinging words being hurled at him,
Boogie turned and faced the mouth of the cave for
the first time in his life.

"Go!" the others yelled.

Choking back his tears, Boogie ran away from his
friends, toward the mouth of the cave …

... and out into the bright light
of the world outside.

Chapter 3:
In Which Boogie's
Eyes Are Opened
to the World

Dazed from the shocking attack from the other cave people, Boogie stumbled about outside the cave until he collapsed, exhausted.

For a long time, he just lay there, crying and confused.

Why had his clan turned on him so suddenly and savagely? All he had done was ask some questions which, to him, seemed pretty simple and legitimate.

Finally wiping the tears from his eyes, Boogie looked up.

He gasped.

This outside world was big—bigger than Boogie could ever have imagined.

He saw creatures, amazing and diverse. Some he vaguely recognized from the shadows he had seen in the cave, but their shadows had only hinted at their true beauty.

In awe, Boogie began to explore.

Boogie had been walking and exploring for a long time when, in the distance, he saw what appeared to be a man sitting on the side of a hill.

As he got closer, he could see that it was indeed a man—a very, very old man.

"Hello. My name Boogie," Boogie said, approaching the man.

"And I am *The Seer of Truth and Purveyor of Wisdom Who Sits on the Mountainside*," the man said. "Or *Mike*, if you prefer. Please, sit."

Boogie seated himself next to Mike.

"I see that you have come from a cave," Mike said. "Welcome to the outside world. You are the first to come out. Did you bring others with you?"

"No. Boogie alone. How you know Boogie come from cave?"

"Your grammar is atrocious," the Purveyor of Wisdom said. "Why don't cave people ever use their articles and pronouns? It makes me so crazy."

Boogie blushed, but Mike continued: "I have been waiting for the day when all cave people would again emerge from their caves and repopulate the land."

Boogie was amazed. "Other cave people are living in other caves?" he asked. (He worded his thoughts carefully, for he was now self-conscious about conjugating his verbs.)

"Oh, yes. There are many, many others, living in hundreds of caves, all across this land," Mike said, staring off sadly into the distance. "They never come out. They never learn."

"Why so many choose to live in cave, when world is so much bigger out here?" asked Boogie.

Settling in, Mike answered:
"It all began long ago...."

Chapter 4:
In Which Mike
Tells the Tale of
Two Tribes

66 **I**t started around forty-five minutes into the Neolithic period," Mike said. "Your ancestors all lived together in a large tribe, right here in these fields. Their numbers grew every year. These were happy times.

"But as the numbers increased, these fields could no longer support the people. Food became scarce, and the people went hungry. They realized they would have to branch out if they were to survive.

"The people were desperate. So they came together for a meeting before the elders of the tribe. The wise elders told them: 'Go and build tall towers that will allow you to see as much of the surrounding lands as possible. When we learn more about the lands around us, then we shall know what we must do.'

"So that's what the people did."

Mike paused for a deep breath. He continued:

"After many, many days, the people returned to the elders.

"'Have you built the towers?' the elders asked.

"'Yes we have,' the tribe replied.

"'Have you seen the lands around us?' the elders asked.

"'Yes we have,' the tribe replied.

"'Then what must we do to survive?'

"'We must build collecting baskets and storehouses for food and weaving looms to make tents,' announced one group. 'Only then will we be able to survive in the surrounding lands.'

"But then another group spoke up. 'No, we must build spears, traps, and tools for the hunt. Only then will we be able to survive in the surrounding lands.'

"The first group responded: 'If we waste time building spears and traps and tools for the hunt, the tribe will surely die.'

"The second group said, 'No, if we waste time building collecting baskets and storehouses and weaving looms, *then* the tribe will surely die!'

"Now the elders were confused," Mike said.

"Me too," said Boogie, engrossed. His eyes were wide, and he sucked nervously on a rock. "What happen next?"

"The people got angry, that's what happened next.

"The first group said to the other: 'Weapons are for killing. To build weapons is barbaric. You are barbarians!'

"The second group responded: 'To sit and weave baskets while our people die of hunger is cowardly. You are cowards!'

"And so it went, back and forth:

'Barbarians!'
                    'Cowards!'
'Violent animals!'
                    'Tree-hugging dorks!'"

Although Boogie didn't know exactly what a tree-hugging dork was, Mike's story evoked painful memories of his last moments in the cave. "Evil" and "delusional" were the words his friends had used.

"So *then* what happened?" Boogie asked.

Mike was quiet for a moment, gazing sadly into the distance. Finally he spoke.

"The tribe split. The first group wove their baskets. The second group built their spears. Eventually the people with the spears drove out their fellow tribesmen, who scattered through the hills and hid. Then, those with spears began to argue among themselves. In the end, they turned on one another. It was horrible."

"So they really *were* barbarians and cowards," Boogie observed.

"No. At least, not at the beginning. But it's what they *became.* The labels they placed on each other became reality. Interesting, how that happens, isn't it?" Mike asked.

It certainly was interesting, but Boogie wasn't quite sure he understood it. He decided he would have to think about that.

"So where everybody now?" Boogie asked.

"In caves. Everyone lives in caves," Mike said quietly.

For a long time, Boogie and Mike just sat there, gazing towards the horizon of that vast, empty landscape.

Chapter 5:
In Which the Tale of
Two Tribes Is Explored,
Nearly Giving Boogie
a Migraine

B oogie's mind raced as he tried to grasp Mike's
story of the two tribes. He thought back to his
experience in his own cave. It somehow seemed
relevant to all of this … but he wasn't sure how. He
wished his pre-evolutionary neo-cortex were more
evolved. Maybe then he could fully understand the
meaning of Mike's story.

Finally, Boogie asked: "So, why tribe disagree at
beginning, anyway? Why divide over spears and
baskets? Boogie not understand."

The old man's eyes sparkled. "Ah. Very good question,
Boogie. Let's go back to the beginning. Why do *you*
think they disagreed?"

Boogie mulled this over for a few moments.
Finally, he replied:

"Not sure, but …
maybe was like shadows on wall."

Boogie could tell that the Seer of Truth didn't quite understand. Boogie continued:

"Well," he said, choosing his words carefully, "maybe everyone see world wrong—like seeing shadows. We see wrong, so we act wrong."

"Very good, Boogie," said Mike. "But perhaps it's not a matter of seeing *wrong*, but of seeing *incompletely*. And that's what happened with our ancestors. Follow me and I'll show you."

Boogie and Mike walked several miles to the far east side of the field. There, they came upon one of the old towers their forefathers had built so many years ago. It was weathered and ramshackle, but still standing.

"Go up and see," said Mike.

Carefully, Boogie climbed the crumbling stone stairs that spiraled to the top of the tower.

From the top of the tower, Boogie could see the eastern horizon. It was coarse, rocky land, populated with buffalo, elk, and sheep.

Boogie could see how, in a land this rich with wildlife, you would certainly need spears, traps, and tools for hunting.

His brow furrowed, Boogie descended the tower and rejoined Mike. "Follow me," Mike said again.

They walked several more miles in the opposite direction. They came upon another crumbling, weathered tower—this one looking out to the west.

Boogie climbed the tower.

From the top of the tower, Boogie could see the western horizon. Unlike the eastern landscape, this was lush land, covered with grape vines, corn stalks, and wild cotton bushes.

Boogie could see how, in a land this rich with vegetation, you would certainly need baskets and storehouses and weaving looms.

Now Boogie understood why the two tribes went to war. Two different towers; two different views.

"We only see in part...." he whispered to himself. He stood there, deep in thought, for a long time.

Finally, Boogie emerged from the base of the tower. He seemed frustrated.

"It all seem so silly," he said to Mike. "Why divide? Why fight over different views? Why not just go in each other's towers, so everyone understand how other sees different?"

"It does seem pretty simple, doesn't it?" answered Mike. "But it seldom works that way. Instead, people divide and work against each other. Why do *you* think this happens?"

Boogie wasn't sure. But it did appear that people became awfully upset when asked about their beliefs, or when somebody suggested there might be other ways to look at things. Soon came the labels ... like *mad,* or *barbarians,* or *cowards....* And after that, came the bruising ashtrays and murderous spears.

Boogie decided this was another important thing to think about.

Suddenly, Boogie turned from Mike.

"Boogie go back now," Boogie said.

"Where are you going?" asked Mike.

"Back to cave. Must tell others what I have seen. No more dividing; no more hiding in caves; no more eating cereal made of gravel.

"Must give others chance to climb more towers. Must all work together to see more truth. Then we can be great in number again. We can eat meat, and drink wine, and make shelter, and populate all of this land."

"Be careful," Mike warned him. "Remember how painful it was for a curious caveperson like you to leave the cave. Imagine how much harder it will be for the others, who are satisfied to stay there."

"Others not be satisfied when I tell them about great big world, and show new way to see," Boogie said, as he turned to leave. "Others will want to learn more, see more."

"Boogie! Wait…!" Mike called after Boogie.

But Boogie was already gone.

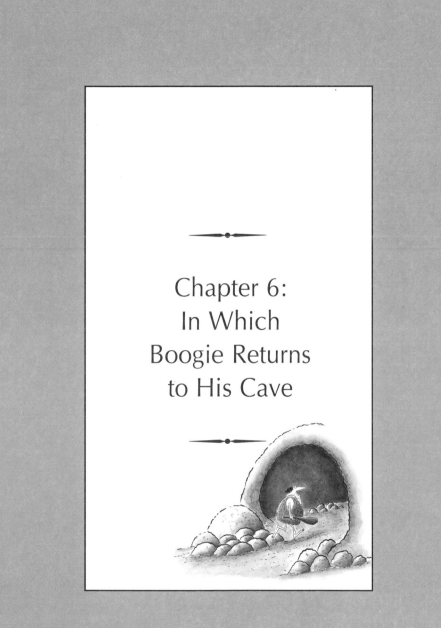

Chapter 6:
In Which
Boogie Returns
to His Cave

After walking many miles, Boogie approached the mouth of his old cave.

From deep inside the cave, Boogie could hear the muffled voices of Unga, Bunga, Oogie, and Trevor, and the familiar crunching sounds as they snacked on dead locusts. (It suddenly occurred to Boogie how gross this really was.)

Boogie's heart ached with sadness and fear. Would his friends turn violent as they had once before? Would they attack him for telling them about the shadows, and the great world he had seen outside the cave?

Or would they be open to joining Boogie in exploring the things they all believed?

Trembling, Boogie took a deep breath.

If they no want to learn, Boogie thought as he stepped into the cave, *I find others who will.*

After all, he thought, *Mike said there were many others, living in hundreds of caves …*

... but really, there were millions.

The End

A Closer Look at *Shadows of the Neanderthal*

Wait—don't close the book quite yet.

You may be thinking, "Ugh ... this last part doesn't look like it's as much fun to read as the first part." That's okay. If you wish to skip this portion of the book and enjoy the story on its own terms, you're welcome to do so. Metaphors hold real power when the reader is allowed to discover their meanings at his or her own pace.

However, deep learning often works best when it is accompanied by *reflection* and *experimentation*. That's what the following pages are for. This section will facilitate your own reflection as you explore the themes presented in *Shadows of the Neanderthal*. So the choice is yours: Feel free to simply enjoy the story "as is," or dive in deeper for some personal exploration.

Still reading? Then like Boogie, you have an appetite for deeper understanding! This is a path that can lead to richer awareness of our complex human experience. But be forewarned that for the next few minutes, we're going to be examining your thinking and exploring the ways you perceive and interpret your world. As Boogie learned, this can be hard to do. If you come up against any unsettling feelings, stay with them—real learning is just on the other side!

Shadows and Light

Shadows of the Neanderthal is really a story about *mental models*—a term coined in the 1940s by Scottish psychologist Kenneth Craik. Here is *our* definition: *"Mental models are the deeply held beliefs, images, and assumptions we hold about ourselves, our world, and our organizations, and how we fit in them."*

This is not abstract, academic stuff. It's a simple idea, really. And it's full of implications for our businesses, our families, our churches, our schools, and all other areas in our lives, since we always need to get along with other people who see things differently from us.

Nor is this a new idea. In his famous dialogue *The Republic,* the Greek philosopher Plato tells The Parable of the Cave, in which a group of subterranean people mistake the shadows they see in the cave for reality. In Plato's original telling of the story, when one of the people discovers the truth about the source of the shadows and attempts to share his knowledge with the others, they rise up and slaughter him. Plato's conclusion to his story is a chilling one: We are *all* misguided cave dwellers, Plato says, operating under incomplete or distorted perceptions of reality ... and violently resistant to having those perceptions challenged.

Ouch. This opens the door to some difficult questions—questions like:

- *Hey—what's so wrong with the way I see the world?*

- *Why do so many people reject the truth, when the truth seems so obvious?*

- *What does this really have to do with me or my organization, anyway?*

Let's answer that last question first. The discussion of this idea is important because mental models limit our organizations every day. Organizational case studies abound of good ideas that never got off the ground, simply because they didn't match the prevailing assumptions or beliefs. One popular illustration is of the Swiss watch industry, which dominated the world market for watches for many years. When the new quartz technology was first introduced, the Swiss manufacturers rejected it, since it didn't match their *mental model* that watches should be mechanical, "ticking" devices—rather than high-tech ones. Instead, Japanese manufacturers like Seiko adopted the new technology, and rapidly took much of the world market from the Swiss. The Swiss fall in the global watch market can be traced back to their dependence on their mental models about what made watches desirable.

Perhaps you have experienced highly politicized conflicts in your organization—conflicts in which people are polarized into factions, each one claiming that the other is short-sighted or self-serving. Look into the heart of such conflicts, and you'll often find different sets of assumptions at work.

Even in religious movements that strive for unity and love, people often find the gulf of separation between themselves and others becoming wider and wider. (Ironically, history is rife with war atrocities that have been committed in the interest of divine love.) These same dynamics may be observed in our families. Again, our mental models are key culprits in such conundrums.

Let's take a closer look at our mental models, and the power that they hold.

Seeing, Believing, and Mental Models

So, what *is* a mental model, really? And how does it function? Here are seven principles that can help illuminate the concept:

Principle # 1: Everyone has mental models.
You have mental models about how the world works. It is impossible *not* to have mental models. As cognitive theorist Edward DeBono illustrates, your mental models are the result of a physiological process in which the neural networks of your brain work to categorize and organize the endless stream of complex information you take in every day. If your mind didn't perform this function, you would be confused every time you saw a car of a different make and style. But fortunately, your mind is efficient enough to say, "Oh, look—there are wheels, windows, headlights … that must fall into the brain category labeled 'car'!" Remember that a mental model is neither a good nor a bad thing—it's just your brain's way of creating order out of this complicated world. The trouble occurs when our brains do their job *too* well, and we force-fit everything we see into categories that worked for us in the past.

Note that individuals aren't the only ones with mental models. When individuals are organized together, the groups and organizations they form *also* develop mental models. Organizations, families, governments ... they are all governed by the collective, deeply held beliefs and assumptions of individuals. In the United States, one collective mental model that is a basis for the very society is the right to "the pursuit of happiness." Virtually all Americans feel entitled to happiness, because they think of it as an "unalienable right." Few have ever thought to challenge the truth of this statement. This is a mental model that has real impact on Americans' daily lives, driving many careers, relationships, and even lawsuits. (Note that there are numerous societies where this expectation of happiness *isn't* part of the collective mental model.)

Principle # 2: Mental models determine *how* and *what* we see.
Our perceptions aren't as clear as we'd like to believe. Everything we perceive must first pass through our filters of mental models. And if something doesn't match the "road map" in our head, we may simply become blind to it.

One colleague conducts this exercise in Western culture training programs: She asks participants in the classroom to study her face and describe her facial features. Typically, participants will describe her nose, hair, eyes, lips, etc. But after conducting this exercise countless times, not one participant has ever mentioned the little divot-shape area between her nose and upper lip. In the West, there is no commonly used word for that part of our faces ... and as a result, people simply don't see it. (When was the last time you noticed this feature on your spouse's or best friend's face?)

I recently saw a photograph of a densely populated downtown street in the city of Hong Kong. Because I am an American, most of the information in the picture appeared to me as a confusing jumble of street signs, shop windows, and neon, all in alien Chinese symbols. However, despite the complexity of the photograph, I noticed how my eyes were almost instantly drawn to a small sign in the photo bearing the familiar McDonald's golden arches logo. In a world of chaotic information, the mind instantly locks onto that which it already knows—and simply filters out other data.

It's a disconcerting thought, but there are truths and rich opportunities that are off-limits to us, simply because they do not match our mental models. At the end of the *Shadows* story, we discover that the cave people are actually living in contemporary times. Yet Boogie remained unaware of the cityscape that existed just beyond his rudimentary cave. (Perhaps it was Boogie's mental models that had inhibited his own evolution while other parts of the world progressed!) To some extent, each of us also lives in a cave, blind to a bigger world just outside our radar screen of perception.

For your reflection:

- Think of a comment that a spouse, partner, or colleague has made about you that you found disturbing or frustrating. After reflecting on the comment, do you find that there is any truth in it? How hard was it initially for you to consider that the comment may be accurate? How is the comment inconsistent with your own deeply held beliefs about yourself?

- Have you ever known anyone with behaviors or traits that were very obvious to others, but seemingly invisible to that person? Why do you think this was so? Might you have similar blind spots about yourself, because they don't match your self-perception?

Principle # 3: Mental models guide how we *think* and *act*.
In the story, Boogie began questioning his own thinking when he asked, "What if we not see what really is?" The initial mental model held by the cave people was, "There is no possible existence beyond this cave." This affected their *thinking*, which eventually resulted in the development of their personal belief systems (like "a big mad god lives outside the cave"). Their mental model also affected their *actions:* They stayed in the cave without ever leaving, even if it meant eating bugs and sucking on rocks. For better or worse, our own mental models limit the range of behaviors we tend to take.

Numerous business case studies illustrate this phenomenon. For example, from 1915 to 1955, the only way one could purchase Coca-Cola (other than at a soda fountain) was in the famous 6 1/2–ounce "contour" bottle that had played such a critical role in the soft drink's early marketing success. The 6 1/2–ounce contour bottle was treated as sacred to the brand's identity, and was widely held to be the "only way" to sell Coke. Coke refused to change for many, many years, even as it lost market share to Pepsi. It was only after deep losses that the company became open to changing its mental model and exploring the possibility of other packaging (like the 12-ounce size).

Likewise, many companies have made history by introducing *new* mental models. Federal Express and Apple Computer developed products and services that many people thought no one would ever want. Dell Computer, too, has changed people's mental models about how computers can be distributed and sold.

For your reflection:

- Think of a time (either personally or organizationally) when you did not get the results you wanted. What were the actions you took that led to those results, and what was your thinking at the time that caused you to take those actions? (It may be easier to reflect on this with a friend, because it is often hard to see our own mental models.)

- Think of a time when you or a group you were associated with excelled by adopting a new mental model.

Principle # 4: Mental models lead us to treat our inferences as facts. To Boogie, the warring tribes' conflict seemed absurd. Surely they could have avoided war and resolved their differences simply by saying, "Hey—wait a minute! There are two different towers with two different views! We are each looking at different parts of the landscape, from different perspectives!"

But maybe it isn't so absurd. The metaphor is correct: We rarely report our conclusions about the "landscape" as our own mental models. Instead, we simply state what we see as if it were fact. In reality, our beliefs seem so obvious to us that we are often amazed that others can see things so differently. Our beliefs remain closed to challenge, and the mental model stays tacit, or hidden.

Imagine a manufacturing plant where there is growing tension between hourly workers and management. Note that a manager probably would not say, "*I have a mental model that* the hourly employees aren't very hard workers." Instead, the manager is more likely to just say, "The hourly employees aren't very hard workers." That's a big difference. By not acknowledging that his belief is merely his own mental model, he makes it difficult for himself and others to examine that belief. By stating "They aren't very hard workers" as fact, the manager creates a situation where it is unlikely that any change will occur.

As we shall see, the lifelong challenge of mental models is identifying them and bringing them out into the light, where they can no longer exercise their hidden power over us.

For your reflection:
- Think of a time when someone presented their mental model as if it were fact. What kinds of responses did this elicit? Can you think of a time when *you* have done this?

- The next time you are personally offended or frustrated by someone's comments, what questions could you ask to better understand the other person's mental models? How could you help him or her do the same for you?

Principle # 5: Mental models are always incomplete.
None of us has a complete perception of the world. The world is much too complicated a place, and none of us can take in that much data and still function. Therefore, what we *do* take in is incomplete.

Like the warring people in the story, each of us has built a tower with its own unique view of the landscape. We all live in different towers with different views—and yet we behave as if everyone should see things the same way we do. Two people may engage in a heated exchange on the politics of abortion, for example, and never come to agreement. They are in different towers with different views, drawing different conclusions about the same landscape—each becoming more incredulous that the other does not see things his way.

When incomplete mental models clash in this way, don't be surprised if each person involved becomes agitated or defensive. You may have experienced this yourself if, for example, anyone ever critiqued the validity of your parenting style, or if someone from a distant department in your organization suggested you should do your job in a different way. Often, when our mental models are challenged or suggested to be incomplete, it's as if someone has pulled the rug out from our very understanding of our world—and our instinct to protect our worldview can be very aggressive.

History provides us with numerous examples of people with radically different mental models who revealed the limitations of existing mental models and faced rejection, imprisonment, or even death. When Galileo first suggested that the earth revolved around the sun, this had tremendous implications for the church-run government of the time, which believed that the earth was the literal, physical center of the universe. In 1633, Galileo was sentenced to life imprisonment for suggesting an incompatible mental model. Likewise, consider the stories of Martin Luther King, Jr., Jesus Christ, or the countless individuals who, even today, are punished for speaking out against the way things are.

For your reflection:
- Consider the "different towers with different views" metaphor as it applies to your own life. What "towers" do you inhabit? It may help you to think in terms of your beliefs about how organizations should be run, beliefs about leadership and motivation, political ideology, theology, parenting style, etc.

- How have your beliefs led to disagreements or impasses with others who inhabit "different towers with different views"?

Principle # 6: Mental models influence the results we get, thereby reinforcing themselves.

Once we adopt a belief about the world, it becomes more and more ingrained, as we continually "select" (or see) only the data that support that belief.

Here's another Coca-Cola story: Ever wonder what drove The Coca-Cola Company to introduce the ill-fated New Coke? This was a case of self-reinforcing mental models. In the 1980s, the cola market was stagnant. Leaders within Coca-Cola believed it was because consumers were tired of the taste of Coke. Sure enough, market research and product testing confirmed this suspicion as the heavily tested New Coke beat out old Coke 5-to-1 in taste tests. But the initial assumption—that people were tired of old Coke—affected which questions the researchers asked, which in turn led to confirmation of their original belief. (Notably, researchers did *not* ask the critical question: "What would you think if we *replaced* Coke with this new product?" Such a question would have revealed the fierce consumer loyalty to the 99-year-old brand. However, the question was never asked because it wasn't consistent with the mental model that assumed consumers were tired of the taste of Coca-Cola.)

Individuals experience this self-reinforcing phenomenon all the time. Let's say that you have come to believe that "teenagers are troublemakers." Thus, every time you observe a teenager engaged in behaviors that you perceive as "trouble-making," that information sticks out. "Ah-hah!" your mind says, seizing on the familiar piece of data. "See? Teens really *are* trouble! I knew it!" On the other hand, when you observe a teen in an act of generosity, you simply disregard it (like the signs printed in Chinese in the photograph) or pass it off as being the exception and not the rule.

But that's just the beginning. Once we hold a belief and continually "select" data from the world that reinforces that belief, *then our experience can begin to conform to make that belief a self-fulfilling reality.*

Remember in the story that Mike observed how the "barbarians" and "tree-hugging dorks" actually *became* what the other perceived? To examine how this happens, let's return to our example of the person who believes that "teenagers are troublemakers." As the person's mental model becomes more deeply held, it will affect his behaviors ... perhaps causing him to approach teenagers he meets tentatively, or even abrasively. This will prompt teens to respond to him aggressively or obnoxiously, which now adds very real evidence to support the original belief system. The person is now in a spiraling pattern of experience driving perception, and perception driving experience. This pattern can be very, very hard to break.

This principle holds true in organizations, too. A company that believes the marketplace is saturated will find few marketing opportunities; another that believes that every associate is capable of producing innovative ideas will tap into a deep wellspring of innovation.

Here's the moral: The way we *see* the world affects our *experience* of the world. When the way we see the world changes, we can then change our role in the world and get very different results. Herein lies the key to remarkable and enduring change.

For your reflection:
• How can this self-reinforcing dynamic help in understanding racism? Generational conflicts? "Problem children" in a family full of achievers? Companies that don't change, even though they're losing customers?

Principle # 7: Mental models often outlive their usefulness.
Don't come to the conclusion that all mental models are irrational. At the time you formed the mental model, it served a very real function. An individual who believes "teenagers are troublemakers," for example, may have developed that mental model at a time when, as a child, he was bullied by an older kid. The mental model served an important purpose in the child's ability to handle very real circumstances.

But problems occur when the mental model becomes outdated and the individual continues to hold on to it. As time goes on, the "teenagers are bad" script is still playing, even though it is no longer necessary. That person's perception of reality is now distorted, like shadows on the wall.

That's why mental models must be updated to be effective. We need to periodically surface and examine our mental models, to see whether they still serve a useful function. We may find that some of our existing mental models are still accurate and valuable reflections of reality. But we will also certainly discover others that are distorted and that no longer accurately reflect reality.

Every few years, science produces a new discovery that forces a dramatic reexamination of current beliefs and assumptions. One such discovery took place just as this book was being developed, in which scientists found that the smallest subatomic particle, called a *neutrino*, has a measurable weight and mass. This is hugely significant, since it was always widely accepted that neutrinos had *no* weight or mass. This stunning revelation has scientists scrambling to reconsider the fundamental nature of matter ... and even reexamining whether the Big Bang was possible. For many years, the old belief about neutrinos served scientists well as they sought to understand our universe. But now that a more accurate mental model has become available, many are having to go "back to the drawing board" and develop new theories.

As you can imagine, this process of updating mental models can be painful. In this age, many organizations find themselves in an uncertain (or even turbulent) environment. Here's one common scenario that you may recognize: As the need for change grows more urgent, factions polarize within the organization, with the "conservatives" fighting to retain the "identity" or "way it has always been" in the organization, while the "liberals" proclaim a "change or die" message. In no time, unexamined mental models are whizzing by like bullets, and casualties begin mounting. It is at such moments that an overt and skillful exploration of current mental models is crucial. But once people become defensive and trigger happy, the possibility for this kind of dialogue is slim.

71

Up the Ladder and into the Cave

Mental models are built over time, incrementally, as we observe data and draw conclusions every day. By understanding how this happens, we can begin to achieve some mastery over this hidden process.

"The Ladder of Inference" is a helpful tool for understanding how our mental models are formed. The ladder is a tool of Action Science, developed by theorists Chris Argyris and Donald Schön, that traces the mental processes (or "leaps of inference") that lead us to form and maintain mental models. The steps are as follows (begin reading at the bottom of the ladder, with step 1, and then read upwards):

The Ladder of Inference

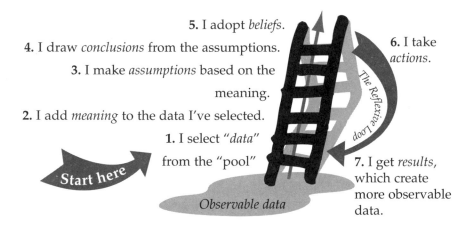

5. I adopt *beliefs.*

4. I draw *conclusions* from the assumptions.

3. I make *assumptions* based on the meaning.

2. I add *meaning* to the data I've selected.

1. I select *"data"* from the "pool"

6. I take *actions.*

The Reflexive Loop

7. I get *results,* which create more observable data.

Start here

Observable data

Consider the experience of Boogie's cavemates, right before they drove Boogie from his home. Here is how their interaction might be traced up the Ladder of Inference:

- The group begins at the foot of the ladder, surrounded by observable data about the world. (Unga, Bunga, Oogie, Boogie, and Trevor are all hanging out in the cave, painting on walls, eating, etc.)

- Then they zero in on a specific piece of data. ("Boogie is saying that he wonders what is outside of the cave.")

- They add meaning to the data. ("Boogie saying we wrong.")

- They make assumptions. ("Boogie lost his mind." "Boogie delusional and narcissistic!")

- They draw conclusions. ("Boogie want to ruin everything!")

- They adopt beliefs. ("This could be end of us!")

Now they take a spin around the Reflexive Loop, the portion of the ladder that reinforces mental models:

- They take actions. (They order Boogie to get out of the cave, and throw ashtrays at him.)

- They get results. (Boogie leaves the cave and seems to disappear.)

- The results of their actions influence which data they "select" the next time. (We can imagine that, after Boogie is driven from the cave, the others might eventually say, "See? Boogie didn't come back. He must have been stomped on by a god/breathed on by a dragon/etc. We were right!")

The leap of inference illustrated above took place within a conversation among the cave people. More typically, the process of racing up the ladder occurs within our subconscious thoughts, almost instantaneously. For example:

- I select data: "When I proposed an idea in the Monday morning staff meeting, no one said anything."

- I add meaning: "There is no follow-up to anything I am saying."

- I make assumptions: "No one appreciates my ideas, or how valuable I could be to this team."

- I draw conclusions: "I'd better not say anything else during meetings."

- I adopt beliefs: "I must not be competent."

Here, my progress up the ladder kicks the Reflexive Loop into gear:

- •I take action. (I stop speaking in meetings.)

- •I get results. (People stop looking to me for input. I then notice this "data" and decide that my belief is true—that I am not competent.)

We make these leaps of inference instantly and silently ... even multiple times in the course of one simple interaction. Over time, these leaps, combined with the action in the Reflexive Loop, crystallize our complex mental models of the world.

Now try the exercise on your own. Review the conflict between the two warring tribes (the barbarians and the tree-huggers, on pages 35–38.) Trace their progress up the ladder and around the Reflexive Loop. Then try to recall a leap of inference that *you* have made in recent experience. Trace your own thinking in the same way.

Out of the Cave and into the Light

Insight alone does not produce change. The fact that you now understand some of the mechanics behind mental models is not a remedy for any undesirable effect they may have in your life and organization. Instead, you must *do* something with your awareness. Learning takes place in a realm of action.

When we are dealing with difficult and threatening problems in organizations, we need to limit the likelihood that our mental models will constrain our ability to take effective action. We can do this by illuminating their presence, and by taking deliberate steps to challenge our thinking against the Ladder of Inference. This is a skill that requires practice. Here are some guidelines, developed by the partners of Action Design (Diana Smith, Bob Putnam, and Phil McArthur), for making your and others' thinking processes explicit:

- Notice that your conclusions may be based on *your* inferences, and that they may *not* be self-evident facts.

    "I think that a big dragon lives outside. But that's *my* belief. I wonder what the others would have to say about that...."

- Assume that your reasoning process could have gaps or errors that you do not see.

    "I think I will disappear if I leave the cave. I wonder if there is any other possibility."

    "Is it possible that those strange shadows and shapes on the wall have an origin that I'm not aware of?"

- Use examples to illustrate the data you selected that led to your conclusions.

    "The reason I think we should build spears and hunting tools is that I looked out the window of the east tower and saw a lot of wild animals."

    "I'm wondering what is outside the cave, because bugs keep coming in here. So my reasoning is that *something* must be out there."

- Paraphrase (out loud) the meanings you hear in what others say, so that you can check if you are understanding correctly.

    "Do I understand correctly that you think the other guys are barbarians because they want to build spears, and you consider the use of spears to be barbaric?"

- Explain steps in your thinking that take you from the data you select and the meanings you paraphrase to the conclusions you reach.

    "I guess the reason I called you delusional and narcissistic is I have a strong belief that a big dragon lives outside the cave. So when I hear you ask out loud what would happen if we left the cave, I guess I almost take it personally ... as if you were challenging the things I believe. I interpret that as a lack of respect, which I don't think was your intention. Can you help me understand what you were saying? Do you have some other line of thinking I'm not aware of?"

"Here are some things that I saw or heard that led me to this conclusion: (state data)."

"In coming to this conclusion, I made an assumption that...."

• **Ask others if they have other ways of interpreting the data or if they see gaps in your thinking**.
"How do you see it differently?"

"What are some flaws in my reasoning that you can see?"

"One thing you can help me think through better is...."

"Do you think that building spears and hunting tools is a good thing to do? Is there anything I'm missing?"

• **Assume that others may reach different conclusions because they have their own Ladder of Inference with a logic that makes sense to them**.
"Obviously, you can see that I am a strong proponent of building spears. But I'd like to hear from someone who has a different take on this. Did anyone come to a different conclusion?"

• **Ask others to illustrate the data they select and the meanings they paraphrase**.
"Can you tell me more about why you say there is a big mad god outside the cave?"

"What did you see in the surrounding lands that you think warrants the building of baskets?"

• **Ask others to explain the steps in their thinking**.
"What leads you to your conclusion?"

"Can you help me understand your thinking here?"

"I wonder if we are making an assumption here, that ... (state assumption)."

"How did you come to the conclusion that I am a barbarian? What did you see that led you to that belief?"

"What leads you to say that I am narcissistic?"

Some of these examples may seem laborious or awkward to you. But with practice, such exchanges flow surprisingly well. Conversation becomes an exciting and meaningful activity, in which shared mental models lead to greater awareness and learning, rather than polarization and stalemate. Yes, it's hard work ... but very necessary if we are ever to increase our collective understanding of ourselves, each other, and our organizations.

Lessons About Mental Models: A Summary

Mental models are deeply held beliefs, images, and assumptions we hold about our world, ourselves, and our organizations, and how we fit in them.

The way we see the world affects our experience of the world. When the way we see the world changes, we can then change our actions and get very different results

Seven Principles About Mental Models:
1. Everyone has mental models.
2. Mental models determine *how* and *what* we see.
3. Mental models guide how we *think* and *act*.
4. They lead us to treat our inferences as facts.
5. They are always incomplete.
6. They influence the results we get, thereby reinforcing themselves.
7. They often outlive their usefulness.

We form mental models by climbing the Ladder of Inference:

1. We select *"data"* from the "pool" of observable data.
2. We add *meaning* to the data we've selected.
3. We make *assumptions* based on the meaning.
4. We draw *conclusions* from the assumptions.
5. We adopt *beliefs*.

The Reflexive Loop reinforces our mental models:

6. Based on the conclusions and beliefs we reach at the "top" of the ladder, we take *action*.
7. We then get results, and those results influence what data we select in the future—thereby reinforcing our original mental model.

Questions and Activities for Group Discussion

Exploring new understandings with others can powerfully enhance learnings that we gain through individual reflection. In that spirit, here are some questions and activities designed to get you talking with your colleagues about the concepts in this book—and thinking about how to use these ideas to make a difference in your own organization. Note: When we use the word *organization* below, we mean your team, department, or entire company. Feel free to explore these questions and activities together on any or all of those levels.

- What are some mental models that your organization may hold about its role in the world?

- How might you and your colleagues begin surfacing and testing some of your organization's mental models?

- What are some of your organization's biggest challenges? How might untested mental models be contributing to the problem?

- Cite some examples of times that your organization has set in motion a self-fulfilling prophecy, in which the group's belief in something actually made that something come true.

- Review the material on the Ladder of Inference, on p. 72. With your colleagues, cite a recent conflict that took place in your organization, in which one of you hastily climbed up the ladder and "jumped" to conclusions about someone else. Replay the conflict by carefully tracing each step up the ladder. In what ways (if any) do the individuals involved see the conflict (and each other) differently after this exercise?

- Review the guidelines for making your thinking explicit (the bullet points on pp. 75–77). Once again, discuss with your colleagues the conflict that you explored above. This time, practice asking the kinds of questions and making the kinds of statements shown on pp. 75–77—in which you and your colleagues make your thinking about the conflict explicit. Try this exercise for a half-hour; is this way of talking starting to feel more natural to you?

Suggested Further Reading

———•———

- Chris Argyris, *Action Science* (Jossey-Bass, 1985). (Introduces a revolutionary theory of organizational inquiry that demonstrates ways to solve problems, enhance human development and learning, and promote individual, organizational, and social change.)

- Chris Argyris, *Knowledge for Action: A Guide to Overcoming Barriers to Organizational Change* (Jossey-Bass, 1993). (The author translates the powerful theoretical approach he introduced in Action Science into practical advice for researchers and managers.)

- Edward DeBono, *I Am Right, You Are Wrong* (Penguin Books, 1991). (An exploration of the ways our brains perceive and process information, and the implications to ourselves and institutions in our society. An inviting and highly accessible read.)

- Peter M. Senge, *The Fifth Discipline: The Art and Practice of the Learning Organization* (Doubleday, 1990). (Explores the five disciplines of the learning organization, with systems thinking as the cornerstone.)

- Peter M. Senge, et al., *The Fifth Discipline Fieldbook* (Doubleday, 1994). (Contains case studies and practical advice from leaders in the organizational learning field.)

Acknowledgments

I would like to express my appreciation to the following friends and colleagues for shaping and guiding this manuscript. You are all teachers to me:

Teresa Hogan, a dear friend, mentor, and Seer of Truth who has provided direction and clarity in my life far too many times to count. Your inspiration is all over these pages;

Bobby Gumbert, who draws from a bottomless well of creativity. Thank you for breathing life into these stories with your illustrations;

LouAnn Daly, for giving so much of yourself to this project, and for thinking with utter precision and and clarity;

Laurie Johnson of Pegasus Communications. You provide wisdom, insight, balance, and fun (and a fair measure of patience);

Renee Moorefield, of The Coca-Cola Learning Consortium, for coaching and inspiring me to "trust the process" again;

Gary Key for deep and challenging discussions on the nature of *truth* and *perception*;

Phil Mooney, archivist for The Coca-Cola Company, for the illuminating case studies;

Ginny Wiley, Kellie Wardman O'Reilly, Rod Williams, Daniel Kim, and all the other "Pegasi" for your energy and belief;

Phil McArthur, Don Seville, and *Greg Hennessy* for taking the time to comment on the manuscript, and for providing valuable insights;

And most of all, my wife *Robbie* and daughter *Emory*. You fill my days with joy and more joy—a pretty compelling reason to leave my world of words and come up out of the basement every evening.

Other Titles by Pegasus Communications

Visit www.pegasuscom.com for detailed information on—and excerpts from—these titles.

Learning Fables
Outlearning the Wolves: Surviving and Thriving in a Learning Organization
The Lemming Dilemma: Living with Purpose, Leading with Vision

The Pegasus Workbook Series
Systems Archetype Basics: From Story to Structure
Systems Thinking Basics: From Concepts to Causal Loops

The "Billibonk" Jungle Mysteries
Billibonk & the Thorn Patch
Frankl's "Thorn Patch" Fieldbook
Billibonk & the Big Itch
Frankl's "Big Itch" Fieldbook

Human Dynamics
Human Dynamics: A New Framework for Understanding People and Realizing the Potential in Our Organizations

The Pegasus Anthology Series
Reflections on Creating Learning Organizations
Managing the Rapids: Stories from the Forefront of the Learning Organization
The New Workplace: Transforming the Character and Culture of Our Organizations
Organizational Learning at Work: Embracing the Challenges of the New Workplace
Making It Happen: Stories from Inside the New Workplace

Newsletters
THE SYSTEMS THINKER™
LEVERAGE POINTS for a New Workplace, New World

The Innovations in Management Series
Concise, practical volumes on systems thinking and organizational learning tools, principles, and applications.